LYFSGUD

If God Sent You a Text Message

LYFSGUD

If God Sent You a Text Message

Laurel Christensen

DESERET
BOOK

Salt Lake City, Utah

DESERET BOOK is a registered trademark of Deseret Book Company.

Visit us at DeseretBook.com

Library of Congress Cataloging-in-Publication Data

Christensen, Laurel.
   LYFSGUD : if God sent you a text message / Laurel Christensen.
      p. cm.
   Summary: In this short devotional book for LDS girls, the author uses texting to illustrate how God wants us to come to him in prayer and scripture study and personal worship time.
   ISBN 978-1-60641-108-7 (paperbound)
   1. Mormon girls—Religious life—Juvenile literature.   2. Text messages (Telephone systems)—Juvenile literature.   3. Christian life—Juvenile literature. I. Title.
   BX8643.C56C86 2009
   248.8'330882893—dc22   2009005713

Printed in China

10   9   8   7   6   5   4   3   2   1

For my parents, Brent & Larrie

Thanks for teaching me these messages

long before texting was even invented.

And for Hannah

Don't ever forget who loves you.

CONTENTS

INTRODUCTION

Recently I spoke at a youth conference. I had been told that the youth in attendance had their cell phones and had been texting during the message from their stake president the day before. Now, I can text as well as the rest of you (okay, not really, but I'm definitely impressively fast for someone "my age"), but I have to tell you that I just wouldn't dream of texting while I was listening to one of my Church leaders. I just know I'd miss something important. When I heard about this issue, I knew that if I didn't address it right at the beginning of our time together, the youth would do the same to me.

But then I realized it wasn't about me.

And so, as soon as I stood up, I said this:

"I have a message from the Holy Ghost. It's not that God

CAN'T text. It's just that, for now, He chooses not to. And so, if you are texting while we're talking together, there will be little chance you'll be able to get any message that God, through the Spirit, might really want to be giving you. God wants to send you a message. I just worry that you won't hear it while you're texting."

The youth were great. They smiled and almost laughed as if they thought I was clever. Then they put their phones away for the entire time we were together. And you know what? We had a great experience. The Spirit came. They felt it. I felt it. I have no doubt they heard God tell them things they never actually heard *me* say that day.

And the texting was still there when we were through. They hadn't really missed a thing.

That got me thinking: What if God DID choose to text? What if He could get to me just as easily as any of my friends can through the convenience of my cell phone? I never miss a text message . . . but I think I miss messages from Him a little too often.

So, if He could text, or rather if He WOULD text, what would He say? I don't pretend to know, but this book is my imaginative attempt at what some of those text messages might be.

I do know one thing: He is anxious to talk to you. And if texting were His chosen method of communication, He would do it. But, for now, it's not. He wants you to come to Him in prayer and scripture study and personal worship time. So don't let these "text devotionals" be replacements for any of that. If they can just be little reminders of messages He is trying to send you, then they've done their job.

At the end of each devotional, you'll see a "Little Message." These are just a few ideas of how you can implement the devotional in your life. But my hope is that you'll get thoughts and messages beyond what you read on these pages. I trust that your Father in Heaven has other things to tell you—other impressions to give you. There is a "His Message to You" space at the end of each devotional. Use these pages to record the impressions YOU get from the Spirit while you read, promptings about something in your life you could change or do differently. And then maybe you could go back and record what happened in your life as a result of following those impressions.

He has messages of His own waiting for you. I promise He does.

And I can't wait for you to discover what they are!

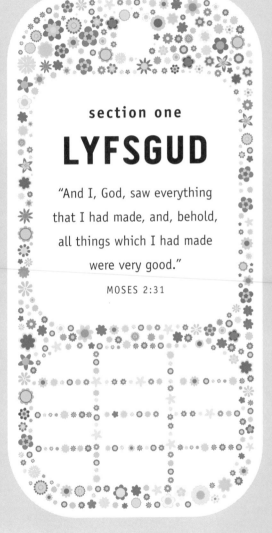

section one

LYFSGUD

"And I, God, saw everything
that I had made, and, behold,
all things which I had made
were very good."

MOSES 2:31

BIG MESSAGE

If I were to ask you to make a "Top 10" list of the things that you love about your life, what would you write? Maybe your list would include things like this:

* My family
* My friends
* The Church
* My talents
* School
* Boys

I spent a lot of my life expecting any and all of those things to be the reasons for loving my life. And consequently, I didn't always love it. Because sometimes my family and I didn't get along; sometimes a friend betrayed me; sometimes I didn't feel connected with the other girls at church; sometimes I did horribly at the speech tournament; sometimes I got a "C" in my favorite subject; sometimes a boy . . . well, you get the idea.

It wasn't until I realized that my life *could* be good and *should* be good just because of who I am—and, more importantly, who my Father is—that everything changed.

I am a "daughter of [my] Heavenly Father who loves [me], and [I] love Him." Do you have any idea what a rare thing that is to know? There are millions of girls, just like you, living all over this planet who don't know that simple truth. Even more sad, they don't even know it's an option. They've never been told that they have a Father in Heaven, let alone that they are His daughters or that He loves them.

I know that truth. I believe it to the very center of my spirit. And knowing it is what makes life so good, even when it's hard . . . even when I'm sad . . . even when things aren't going the way I want them to.

A couple of years ago, I was about as sad as I've ever been. I was dealing with some hard things and I didn't quite know how to get myself out of the funk I was in. I talked to a lot of people and spent a lot of time praying and reading my scriptures and writing in my journal. But for some reason things weren't clicking for me, and I just had this sadness going with me everywhere I went.

Then, I had the chance to get a personalized license plate on my car. It's a silly thing, but I chose the letters: LYFSGUD ("Life's good"). I didn't actually believe it at the time, but I wanted it to be true. I wanted my life to be good . . . *really* good.

At first I thought it might be obnoxious driving around with this little affirmation. But the first day I was driving to work and had to go through a construction area, I got stopped by a woman who didn't look very happy. She was standing in front of my car so a truck could cross the road. She looked down at the license place for a moment. She looked back at me. And then back at the license plate. I think it finally clicked for her. She smiled, gave me a thumbs-up, and then moved out of my way so I could continue to work.

Things like that started happening all the time. I would be in a parking lot and I'd hear a kid say, "Look, Mom. That license plate says 'life's good.'" Or I'd be stuck in traffic and I could see in my rearview mirror the guy behind me reading my plate and trying to figure out what it said. Eventually I would see him shake his head (signaling to me that he thought it was kind of silly), but inevitably he would smile. Maybe he needed the reminder too.

After a while, I noticed the sadness was gone. I know that the reason it left was ultimately because I was praying and reading my scriptures and trying to sort things out. But I also know that part of it had to do with my change in attitude. I started noticing all the ways every day that Heavenly Father was involved in my life, and, before I knew it, my life *was* good (even though nothing else had really changed).

He is God, and everything He made IS good. That includes my very own life.

Life really is good. And it's not because I've been blessed with a perfect family or perfect friends (though if they are reading this, they totally are). And it's not because every Sunday is perfect at Church or everything goes right with work or school . . . or BOYS. But it's good—really, really good—because of this simple truth: I, Laurel Christensen, am a daughter of my Heavenly Father who loves me . . . and I LOVE HIM! I can't help but smile when I say that. It's a pretty great thing to be able to say.

Do you know it? Do you believe it? Let it be the thing that makes your life good . . . no matter what.

✳ little message ✳

Give yourself a little "LYFSGUD" reminder. You might put it on your bathroom mirror or inside your scriptures. You might want to tape a note to your locker. But put it somewhere you can see it every day. And when you read it, put a smile on your face and remind yourself that YOU are a daughter of your Heavenly Father who LOVES YOU. (And let everyone else wonder what that grin is all about!)

His Message to You

section two

GOD LVS U!

"I have loved thee with an

everlasting love . . ."

JEREMIAH 31:3

BIG MESSAGE

My first crush was in the second grade. I would often take a flower and imitate what I had seen in cartoons dozens of times: I would take each petal off one by one and say, "He loves me, he loves me not." And if the last petal was a "he loves me not," I would just go and pick a new flower. I could always find a flower that ended with "He loves me." I always liked those flowers best.

When you repeat with other young women the YW theme: "We are daughters of our Heavenly Father who loves us . . ." that is the only option. There is no "He loves us, he loves us not" game. His love is constant and it's eternal.

I think one of the only people I can remember always, always loving was my grandpa. I don't remember ever not loving him. I don't remember ever being annoyed by him. I don't remember ever saying anything unkind to him (I sadly can't say the same for all the other people I love). And I don't remember ever thinking he didn't love me. And so, because I've felt that way about someone before, and because I know he felt that way about me, I can kind of imagine the love of my Father in Heaven. I know I can't completely comprehend His love, but I can trust that it exists.

I get lots of questions from girls. The big ones always seem to have to do with boys, and the most common question is, "How do I know if he likes me?" I know that question feels so important when you're in the midst of meeting a great new guy who you really like. OF COURSE you hope he likes you too. And trust me, if there was a sure way to tell if that boy likes you too, I would bottle up that formula and sell it.

But, because the answer to that question can be elusive, I like to replace it with another one that I have found is more important. The first, most important question is this: How do you know your Father in Heaven loves you? And I don't mean just kind of cares about you. I mean really, really loves you . . . so much that He probably can't stop Himself from showering you every day with all the blessings He has waiting for you. If you know for sure the answer to whether or not Heavenly Father really loves you, the "does that boy like me?" question becomes just a little less important.

When you repeat every Sunday these incredible words, "We are daughters of our Heavenly Father who LOVES US," do you feel how true that is? Do you see evidence of it all around you?

I'm a believer that God does not love His daughters any more than He loves His sons. But I do believe He loves us just a little differently. He is YOUR Father . . . literally. YOU are HIS little girl . . . literally. In addition to loving you, He wants to teach you and protect you and help you and bless you.

Here are just a few ways He shows me that He loves me:

When I say my prayers in the morning, my day goes better.

When I mess up, He inspires my bishop or another leader to check in with me.

When I need to feel His love, He has a friend call me.

When I ask Him to help me, He prompts my parents to talk to me.

There are proofs of "He loves me" petals all around you. There might be times you question the love of a family member or a friend or a boy, but never ever *ever* question the love of your FATHER in Heaven who loves you . . . desperately. There has never been a moment in time when He wasn't aware of you or when He didn't love you. Never.

I believe nothing is more important than knowing He loves you, because His love gives everything else in life meaning and purpose. The ultimate expression of that love was the sacrifice of His Son, your brother, the Savior Jesus Christ (see John 3:16). That "proof" should be at the top of your list.

So, the next time you pick a flower, remember that there are no "He loves me not" petals where your Father in Heaven is concerned.

HE loves you.

He LOVES you.

He loves YOU.

❊ little message ❊

Start a little "He loves me" journal and for thirty days record all the evidence you see each day of that sacred truth. Make a commitment that anytime you have the chance to repeat the Young Women's theme, you will say that first sentence with a smile on your face . . . because YOU know that YOU are a daughter of our Heavenly Father who LOVES YOU!

His Message to You

BIG MESSAGE

When I was in middle school, I got a new name. I didn't choose this name. I liked my current name and had no need to get a different one. But there was a boy who thought otherwise. His name was Tony and he was . . . horrible.

Now, in fairness to Tony, he was the kid at school who got picked on by the other boys (and a few mean girls). And, like most picked-on kids, Tony had to turn his revenge on someone. For some reason, I was the "lucky" target.

Tony and I had gym class together, and about halfway through the term, he created this mean, albeit somewhat nonsensical, name for me. Nearly every day, he would wait for me to walk out of the girls' locker room and then follow me to where I sat for roll call, all the while saying this name. I could have just rolled my eyes at it, but the worst part (at the time) was that "Jimmy B," who I loved, sat in front of me, and I knew he could hear what Tony was saying. I was embarrassed. Actually, I was in seventh grade—let's face it, I was devastated.

One day, after Tony had followed me to my seat on the gym floor, repeating the name to me over and over again for the umpteenth time, Jimmy B stood up—true story—and grabbed Tony by the shirt and pushed him up against the wall and said, "Don't you ever say that to her again." Isn't that great? I heart you, Jimmy B, wherever you are. To this day, I still heart you for that!

The name bullying finally stopped, thanks to the interference of Jimmy B. But the damage of that name on my little spirit had already been done. I had heard that name over and over again so many times that it kind of stuck with me.

Now, let me shift gears for a minute. There is a great story in the New Testament that you are probably familiar with. Do you remember hearing about the evil spirits that Jesus cast out of a man? And the evil spirits entered the bodies of some pigs, who then jumped off the cliff? I remember hearing that story many times as I was growing up. But I hadn't ever really read the story for myself from the scriptures.

The story is found in Mark, chapter 5. A man, being possessed of many evil spirits, comes to Jesus. Jesus asks the man what his name is, and the man's response is interesting, but also really very sad. The man answers, "My name is Legion: for we are many" (verse 9). Isn't that interesting? He doesn't tell Jesus his real name. He tells him some other name. Perhaps the adversary had been working for so long to discourage him that the man forgot who he really was. He forgot his real name—the name that God knew him by.

Maybe the adversary had been whispering to this man for a long time. Maybe the adversary had been telling him he wasn't good, wasn't loved, wasn't worth anything. Eventually, the man believed it and let Satan overtake him.

I kind of understand a small part of that. For a long time in my life, whenever I would feel insecure or discouraged or afraid, it didn't take much for Tony's name for me to come back into my mind. In those moments, I wasn't "Laurel, one of Heavenly Father's loved daughters" anymore. I was some other girl—a girl not good enough or pretty enough or smart enough or worthy enough to be loved.

Do you have a name that you sometimes call yourself that

doesn't match your real identity? Has someone in your life said something negative about you so many times that you've started to believe it? Maybe you've been told that you aren't pretty enough or smart enough or good enough? Whatever that name (or label) might be, it is NOT who you really are. Don't let any "Tonys" in the world ever tell you that you are anyone else but a "daughter of our Heavenly Father" who LOVES you.

Let that truth be stronger and louder than any other identity someone might try to give you.

In addition to loving you, your Father in Heaven KNOWS you. He knows you perfectly.

And your real name, your real identity, is known to Him.

✳ little message ✳

What if you knew that every time your Father in Heaven talked about you, He referenced a characteristic? What if, instead of calling you by your birth name or some other name you've been given, He referred to you as His "trustworthy daughter" or His "clean daughter" or His "kind daughter"? Write the name you WISH He called you by—and then live as if He already does.

 His Message to You

_____

_____

_____

_____

_____

_____

_____

_____

_____

_____

_____

_____

_____

_____

_____

_____

_____

_____

section three

24/7

"Search diligently,
pray always,
and be believing . . ."

DOCTRINE AND COVENANTS 90:24

BIG MESSAGE

I pray a lot. I'm a girl who prays while I'm sitting at my desk at work or while driving (with my eyes OPEN, of course). I pray out loud. I pray in my heart. I pray while I'm out with my friends or while on a date. (Those are always interesting prayers!) I pray to my Father in Heaven like I'm really talking to Him because I trust that He's really listening. If they handed out grades for praying, I bet I'd get an "A."

But, it turns out I haven't always been praying like I should . . . or like I could.

I was sitting in a Sunday School class listening to a discussion of Alma 34 when I heard verse 26 read out loud:

"But this is not all [Amulek says after discussing all the things we should pray over and all the places we should pray from]; ye must pour out your souls in your closets, and your secret places, and in your wilderness."

And then I began a little conversation with myself.

"Hmmm. Laurel, did you catch that? He said POUR OUT YOUR SOULS."

"Yeah, I do that. Not a problem. Don't you remember that time a few weeks ago when I was driving home late at night and I was crying and I talked out loud while I was praying? If that's not pouring out my soul, what is?"

"Okay, I'll give you that, but He wants you to pour out your whole soul in your closet."

"Check. I've actually physically prayed before, from my closet."

" . . . and in your secret places."

"Check. Check. I've done that, too. I've gone into the bathroom at the office. That's a pretty secret place."

" . . . and in your wilderness."

"Girls camp . . . just a few weeks ago. I even challenged the girls to do it too. You don't get much more 'wilderness' than that! Check. Check. Check."

"I think you're missing the point, Laurel."

And then it happened. Maybe you know what I'm talking about. It's the connection that comes when your heart is finally ready to hear what the Spirit has been trying to tell you. Sometimes we call those "aha" moments.

"What if Amulek's not talking about the place where YOU are? What if this verse is talking about the place where your SOUL is?"

That was when it hit me. Maybe this wasn't an invitation to pray from any specific location. Maybe this was an invitation to pray to my Father in Heaven with all of my heart and be honest with all of my feelings.

Think of your "closets" as those things that you try to hide— your mistakes, your negative thoughts, your negative feelings.

Think of your "secret places" as those things that are most important to you that maybe you never talk about—your concerns about your parents, your desires for the future, the things that make you cry.

Think of your "wilderness" as the things you really wonder about—your testimony, your faith, your fears.

He wants to talk to you . . . REALLY talk to you. And He wants you to talk to Him . . . REALLY talk to Him about all of those things. There is absolutely a need to be formal when we pray. You need to treat your Father in Heaven with absolute respect. But there is also a need for you to feel free to be informal and really share what's in your heart.

Have you ever done that? Have you ever told Him what worries you or what makes you sad? Have you told Him what you really want? Or have you told Him how you need Him to help your family? Have you shared with Him what's hard for you or asked for the help you need in overcoming some of your weaknesses?

You can pray to your Father in Heaven anytime, anywhere. You can pray to Him in seminary class on behalf of all the other students. You can pray to Him in family prayer when it's early and you'd rather be asleep. You can pray to Him in your heart when you're with your friends and you just need a little bit of help being strong. But I hope you'll also pray to Him when you're on your own and you can talk out loud and pray to Him with your WHOLE SOUL. "Pray always" by sharing what's in your heart.

He loves you and is ready to listen . . . to all of it.

⁂ little message ⁂

Someone gave me a challenge once to try to pray for fifteen minutes. I remember looking at the clock with one eye several times. It was hard to find enough things to talk about. But after you've done it a few times, sometimes fifteen minutes isn't nearly long enough. Try it. Set your alarm or a timer for fifteen minutes and don't get off your knees a second early. Stay there and talk to Him. Really talk to Him. And if you run out of things to say, just stay there and listen. Really listen.

His Message to You

BIG MESSAGE

I spent some time once in Toronto (Ontario, Canada) with some friends. In the middle of the downtown, there is a little park surrounded by a major mall and a lot of office buildings. In the middle of the park is a labyrinth made with different colored stones in the cement. A labyrinth is kind of like a maze but it has no dead ends, just a beginning and an ending. And some clever person had created one right in the middle of this park.

There was a sign that explained the labyrinth and its importance in the early days of the city. People believed that if you came into the labyrinth thinking about a question or a problem you were having, by the time you got to the end, you would have figured out the answer. The instructions on the sign told us to simply walk at our own pace while we thought quietly to ourselves.

One of my friends didn't do anything. She just sat in the middle of the labyrinth. My other friend started at the beginning but got bored before she reached the end. I started somewhere in the middle and ended up walking out the entrance. None of us followed the instructions. None of us got an answer.

Now, I don't personally believe in "the power of the labyrinth" or anything like that. But I did have some questions on my mind at the time that I had needed answers to. And the "labyrinth experiment" really taught me something.

Sometimes I'm like my first friend. I want to just sit and not have to really do anything. I just hope the answer will come to me, or the problem will solve itself.

Sometimes I'm like my other friend. I start the process of seeking for my answer but I get tired of trying to figure it out and I give up.

Sometimes—more often than not—I'm like myself. I look for a shortcut (like starting in the middle of the labyrinth) and then end up right back at the beginning.

But when I follow the instructions (just like the labyrinth sign promised), I get my answer. EVERY TIME. It might take more effort and time than I would like, but eventually, I get the answer.

We typically think of using prayer, rather than a labyrinth, to find answers. And prayer absolutely works. In addition to praying for answers, we also are invited to search the scriptures. Someone told me once that prayer is the way we talk to Heavenly Father, and the scriptures are the way He talks to us. The scriptures themselves tell us that within the words of Christ, we can find the answers to anything. "Feast upon the words of Christ; for behold, the words of Christ will tell you all things what ye should do" (2 Nephi 32:3).

Are you willing to do the work to figure out what Heavenly Father wants for you, what He wants you to know?

His instructions are clear:

"You have supposed that I would give it [the answer] unto you, when you took no thought save it was to ask me. But, behold, I say unto you, that you must study it out in your mind; then you must ask me if it be right, and if it is right I will cause that your bosom shall burn within you; therefore, you shall feel that it is right" (Doctrine and Covenants 9:7–8).

There is one thing I know for sure: He has all the answers and He'll give those answers to you as you need them. It might take some time. And even though you and I might not be able to figure everything out, He knows everything. EVERYTHING. He'll help us. He'll answer us . . . as long as we're willing to follow the instructions.

I KNOW that is true.

✳ little message ✳

Start a scripture journal that you use whenever you study the scriptures. Begin with a question that has been on your mind—ANY question about school or your family or your life. Write down the question. Then, when you spend time studying the scriptures, read with your question in mind. Keep a record of your journey and prayerfully ask God to use the scriptures to teach you what you need to understand so that you can get the answer He is waiting to give you.

His Message to You

section four

U READ 2DAY?

" . . . Whoso readeth, let him understand; he that hath the scriptures, let him search them . . . "

3 NEPHI 10:14

BIG MESSAGE

If you had to go a year without your scriptures, how would you feel? Do you use the scriptures enough that you would even notice? Would it impact your life negatively? What about going for five years? Ten years? How much would you be able to remember on your own if you weren't able to refer to the scriptures whenever you needed to?

There's a story in the Old Testament about a time when the people were without the scriptures. The story is in 2 Kings 22.

King Josiah was just eight years old when he began his reign. The story says he was a good young man. But because he had grown up without the influence of the scriptures, he ruled without knowing what the scriptures taught.

When Josiah was eighteen, he sent one of the high priests to put together a crew to repair the temple. During the repair job, Hilkiah, the high priest, found the scriptures hidden within the walls of the temple. He sent them back to be read to the king. "And it came to pass, when the king had heard the words of the book of the law, that he rent his clothes" (verse 11).

The king, upon hearing the words from the scriptures, learned for the first time about the laws that he and his people should have been living. He was overwhelmed with sadness—so overwhelmed that he ripped his clothes! He understood that his people had fallen away from God's truths.

We don't know why the people were without the scriptures for so long that they couldn't study them, why those records had been hidden long enough that the teenage king had never been taught from them. But they *were* lost. And without the scriptures being available, those people simply didn't know the things they needed to know to live the way they needed to live.

What about you?

Your scriptures probably aren't lost. They likely are even sitting on your nightstand next to your bed. But when we go days or weeks or months without studying our scriptures, it's no different from having them "hidden" in the walls of the temple. Just like Heavenly

Father won't force us to *do* anything, He also won't force us to *learn* anything. If we are not reading the scriptures, we simply can't discover what God is waiting to teach us from His word.

Sometimes we get too caught up in the number of pages or the length of time we think we should spend with the scriptures. But even if you can only give scripture study a few minutes a day, it is better than no minutes at all. President Howard W. Hunter taught that "a quarter of an hour [that's fifteen minutes] is little time, but it is surprising how much enlightenment and knowledge can be acquired in a subject so meaningful" (*Ensign*, November 1979, 64). You deserve all the light and truth that will come into your life when you study the scriptures.

You've been talking to Him when you pray.

Let Him talk to you as you read.

❋ little message ❋

Choose a regular spot for your scripture study. It might be in the quiet of your own room or in a favorite chair in the family room. Find a favorite blanket to use only as your scripture blanket. Create a little "study kit" with your scripture journal, a red pencil, and a favorite pen. Make the space cool and have the kit handy so it's easy to just sit and enjoy some quiet time. Try to be consistent by studying at the same time for a few weeks (even if it's just fifteen minutes).

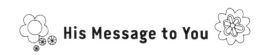

His Message to You

BIG MESSAGE

I fly a lot for work, and I'm always curious who I'll end up next to on the plane. It's often fun to meet someone new and maybe get a chance to have a gospel conversation. I rarely sit beside anyone with whom I can't have an interesting conversation. There are so many good people in the world!

One weekend, after having been out of town several times throughout the month, I was looking forward to flying back home. I sat in my seat and got out my planner, intending to figure out all the great things I was going to do with my time once I was home. A woman came and sat next to me. She was very emotional, and I felt like maybe I should reach out to her.

I asked her name, and she proceeded to tell me a very sad story about how her family had experienced a tragedy and she was on her way to be with them. What was more sad to me was that her speech was very slurred and her eyes were glossed over. I could easily tell that she was under the influence of something.

Shortly after the plane took off, as the flight attendants were starting the beverage service, this woman ordered a drink (not the "soda" kind). I often sit next to people who choose to drink on the flight, but I've never been with anyone who already had been drinking so much. When the flight attendant handed this woman her drink, her hands were so shaky that she spilled a bit of it on herself. I think I might have rolled my eyes in annoyance.

While she was drinking, she started to say some odd things. I tried to be polite but I started to get uncomfortable. Finally she closed her eyes and rested for a little bit. I hoped she would just sleep through the whole flight.

But then she woke up and got another drink. The longer I sat there, the more uncomfortable I became. She was probably harmless, though very drunk, but the uneasy feeling just kept getting stronger and stronger. I wanted to change seats but the flight was full. I was stuck.

Then I remembered my little red pocket-sized copy of the Book of Mormon. I keep it in my bag when I travel so I always have it handy to read (and just in case I need to have one to give away to someone). I stood up and retrieved it from my bag in the overhead compartment. I sat down and held it. There was just something about holding that book that made me feel more comfortable. I felt safe.

I wish there was more to the story. I wish I could tell you that I was filled with the Spirit and started preaching to the woman . . . or that she felt the power of the scriptures and changed her ways. But we didn't really talk much, and I didn't feel impressed to teach her anything. The lesson for me was in the feeling that came over me just from holding that little Book of Mormon in my hands for the rest of the flight.

Right before this flight I'd been teaching a group of Laurels. As part of the lesson, I gave them each a little red pocket-sized Book of Mormon. I invited the girls to keep those books with them so they would have them handy when they had a few minutes to read or had another need for the scriptures. One of the girls was particularly amused by my invitation. (I think she might have even rolled her eyes.) But I was the one who was amused the following Sunday when she said that she went to a dance club with some friends, and when her bag was checked, the guy at the club saw her little Book of Mormon sitting inside her purse. He asked if she was sure she should be at the club. (Interesting, isn't it? that sometimes other people put more stock in the scriptures than we do!)

I like to think the scriptures do more than make us FEEL safe, they KEEP us safe, too. While it's so important that we take time to read them, I'm a believer too that there's power just in having them with us. When it comes to putting on the "whole armor of God," having the scriptures with you becomes the perfect accessory.

✳ little message ✳

Ask your parents to get you one of the small red pocket-sized copies of the Book of Mormon, or get one on your own. It's the perfect accessory for your bag! When you have time at the bus stop or waiting for a friend or at lunch, just get it out and read. You'll be amazed how much it helps just to have the scriptures with you.

His Message to You

section five

B NYS 2 OTHRS

"And be ye kind one to another,

tenderhearted, forgiving

one another . . . "

EPHESIANS 4:32

BIG MESSAGE

I took a calligraphy class once because I thought it would put my doodling skills to good use . . . and because one of the coolest girls I knew was taking the class. I thought I would have a good opportunity to get to know her better if I had a class with her. Little did I know that the class wouldn't have much to do with learning calligraphy OR with the cool girl.

For one assignment we had to choose the lyrics of a children's song or nursery rhyme to create a piece using a whimsical font. One of my favorite children's songs ever is "I'm Trying to Be like Jesus." I didn't want to tackle the whole verse plus chorus so I just chose the following lines:

I'm trying to be like Jesus; I'm following in his ways.
I'm trying to love as he did, in all that I do and say—

Love one another as Jesus loves you.
Try to show kindness in all that you do.
Be gentle and loving in deed and in thought,
For these are the things Jesus taught.

(*Children's Songbook*, pp. 78–79)

I spent a good week on this project. I was so pleased with how it turned out that I ended up matting it on a colorful board to turn in for my final assignment. I took it to class and showed it off. I received my "A" right there on the spot and proudly took my matted project home.

A couple of nights later, in the rain, I was driving down the street and noticed "Jenny" from my class. She was walking with some bags of groceries . . . in the rain. Jenny was really quiet. I wouldn't say I was ever mean to her, but I certainly hadn't taken the time to be nice or to become her friend. My friend and I stayed in our own little clique in that class and weren't overly friendly to the other girls. And so I didn't really know Jenny. Because, after all, she wasn't the "cool girl" in the class that I was trying to get to know better.

When I saw her in the rain, I had this thought that I should pull over and offer her a ride. Immediately I said to myself, "I'm sure she lives nearby. Besides I've never even been nice enough to talk to her in class. It will be weird to offer her a ride."

As I said that, my calligraphy masterpiece, still sitting in my front seat, caught my eye. I didn't even have to read the words on my project. I could feel the Spirit inviting me once again to "be like Jesus," pull over, and offer her a ride.

And so I did.

I rolled down my window.

"Jenny, do you need a ride?"

She turned to me with a confused look on her face.

I felt like I should say, "I'm that 'not mean but not nice' girl in your calligraphy class." But instead I just said, "It's Laurel. I'm in your calligraphy class. Can I give you a ride somewhere?" She very gratefully loaded her groceries in my car and I started taking her home.

The conversation was awkward at first because I had never before made an attempt to even talk to her. I suddenly was embarrassed about that. Who did I think I was? More important, who didn't I realize SHE was? But I started asking her about her life, and by the time we got to her house (which actually would have been a very long walk), I realized she was a really sweet girl. She thanked me and got out of my car.

As I was driving home, I realized that the calligraphy creation sitting in my car hadn't deserved to be on my wall before that night. It was just a nice song, not something I was living. I hadn't been "trying to be like Jesus"; I had been trying to be cool with my friend. I hadn't been showing "kindness in all that you do"; I had been too busy to even pay attention to those around me. I didn't like the girl that I had been in that class, but I was grateful that night for a little reminder of the girl I COULD be in that class.

One of my very favorite quotes of all time is from C. S. Lewis:

"It is a serious thing to live in a society of possible gods and goddesses, to remember that the dullest and most uninteresting person you can talk to may one day be a creature which, if you saw it now, you would be strongly tempted to worship, or else a horror and a corruption such as you now meet, if at all, only in a nightmare. All day long we are, in some degree, helping each other to one or other of these destinations. It is in the light of these over-whelming possibilities . . . that we should conduct all our dealings with one another. . . . There are no *ordinary* people. You have never talked to a mere mortal" (*The Weight of Glory and Other Addresses* [HarperSanFrancisco, 2001], 45–46).

It's okay if you have to read that twice. In fact, go ahead and read it again.

All day long you are interacting with other children of God. You don't know who they really are any more than they know who YOU really are. But they deserve to be treated like you deserve to be treated, and we would all do well to remember that we are helping each other along to be the amazing women (and men) we were born to be.

I can't say that I'm always as nice or as aware of others as I should be. But when I stop to remember the simple truth that everyone is a child of God, it changes the way I treat and interact with others. There are just too many girls like "Calligraphy Laurel" not paying attention to the people around them—not being as nice as we could be. And, sadly, there are too many other girls like "Jenny" just waiting for someone to be kind and help them on their journey down life's rainy streets.

Which girl are you?

Which girl do you want to be?

✳ little message ✳

Choose one weekday when you will focus on "trying to be like Jesus" in ALL of your interactions. Go out of your way to seek out a "Jenny" and befriend someone new, paying special attention to any girls who might be alone. It might help to write the lyrics to that Primary song and keep them in your pocket. (No calligraphy skills needed!)

His Message to You

BIG MESSAGE

When I was a little girl, I had a couple of really faithful friends. They were always there whenever I needed them. They liked to play whatever I wanted to play. They laughed with me and talked to me and were the best friends any little girl could ask for. Their names were Galoboset and Ber-read. Yes, those were the real names . . . of my imaginary friends.

I could tell you the story of how I found them, but you would laugh. (As if you aren't laughing already!) How I found them isn't important, though. What's important is WHY I had them in my life. Even as a young girl I knew how important it was to have good friends; I knew how much I needed them. But in life you need more than imaginary friends . . . you need REAL ones.

My family moved from California to Kentucky when I was ten.

I was a pretty happy girl and I adjusted quickly to my new home. It was the first time I ever had to make friends. At ten years old, though, you're usually excited to be moving and it's a pretty easy age to make friends. To this day, all these years later, I'm still very close with two of the girls I met in fifth grade. I feel very blessed.

Then when I was sixteen we moved from Kentucky to Missouri. I wasn't very happy with my parents for moving me towards the end of high school, and I didn't find the adjustment to be easy at all. In fact, it was downright hard. I had a few girls try really hard to be my friends, but I wasn't very interested. I was too caught up in my own sadness and disappointment over moving.

Eventually, though, because I knew I needed good friends, I opened myself up to my new high school. And thankfully, one of the girls who tried over and over and over again to be my friend was still open to being friends with me. To this day, all these years later, she remains one of my very best friends.

I had good friends in college who have now been with me through a lot of life experiences. They know who they are, and I am eternally grateful for the way they have blessed my life. I have learned how important it is for girls to have really great girlfriends and kind, supportive friends who are boys (which is different from a "boyfriend").

A couple of years ago, I was feeling the need for a good, solid group of girlfriends. I had wonderful friends, but I didn't really have a group, and I was envious of girls who did. So I decided to create one. I looked around and noticed that I knew several great girls and that any one of them would be an added blessing to my life. And I organized a little dinner party so we could all get to know each other.

Now these six girls are my "sisters for life."

I know there are times when it is really important to have friends. And sometimes you're willing to do anything to get them. But I don't even remember anymore some of the "popular" girls who I thought I wanted to have as friends. I don't remember them because those aren't the kinds of friendships that last. The friendships that I still have to this day are with the girls who share my values. I have friends of many faiths, but we have one thing in common: We are daughters of God and we know it.

I got a letter once from a girl who was struggling because she was the only girl in her school who happened to be LDS. She wanted to know what to do about not having any friends. My answer was simple: "Find some." And when she wanted to know how to choose friends, my suggestion was also simple: "Be true to who you are. And then, find girls who know they are daughters of their Heavenly Father who loves them . . . and they love Him."

You are not alone. You are NOT the only girl on the planet who wants to be good. It might feel like that sometimes, but you just have to look harder.

There are lots of good, strong girls out there, and many of them are likely praying for a friend like you. They might not go to church with you, and they might not believe everything you believe, but Heavenly Father is just as aware of them as He is of you. He might even be working to make sure your paths cross. Don't limit yourself to just girls who happen to be LDS. There are other great girls out there who will bless your life and help you choose the right. I'm so grateful that some of my lifelong friends didn't have a rule to befriend only "non-Mormons." I wouldn't have made the cut . . . and we all would have missed out on some really important relationships.

If you're wishing you had more friends, pray for help finding them. Look for girls who look happy, even when no one is around. Look for girls who have the light of Christ and treat others kindly.

Look for girls who will help you be good. I promise they are out there.

And they aren't the least bit imaginary. They are real!

✳ little message ✳

Make a list of qualities you appreciate in a friend. Then make a list of all the girls you know at church and at school. Choose one girl on that list who you think would make a great friend for you. Pray and ask Heavenly Father to help you to get to know her and to have courage (if you need it) to get out of your comfort zone. Be brave and take the first step and invite her to do something. Every attempt won't result in a "best friend," necessarily, but you'll add more friends to your life regardless.

section six

CTR

" . . . ye are free to act for
yourselves—to choose the way
of everlasting death or the
way of eternal life."

2 NEPHI 10:23

BIG MESSAGE

Do you have younger brothers or sisters? Do you remember when they were just starting to talk and ask questions? Do you remember that their favorite question seemed to be "WHY"?

Well, when I was growing up and experiencing all the challenges of high school, my favorite question seemed to be: "WHY be good?"

I remember an experience my senior year. My family had just recently relocated to a new city. I had left behind all of my friends and was anxious to make new ones. I got invited to a party, and though I knew it probably wasn't a party that I should be going to, my desire to make friends was pretty strong. I talked to my parents about it, and my dad told me I shouldn't go. "But," he said, "it's your choice."

I remember being irritated and wondering why I couldn't just go and not even worry about it. Why would it be bad to go to the party? I thought through questions like:

Will I be kept out of heaven if I go to the party?

Will I be kicked out of the Church if I go to the party?

Will I lose my family if I go to the party?

Even if I went to the party and I did something dumb, would this one party really be that big of a deal?

If I had based my decision just on the answers to those questions, I have to say that I would have gone to the party. But you can't make decisions to do what is right based on the logical answers of one situation; the "logical answer" is not always the right answer.

For me, the typical, "logical" answers to the "WHY be good?" question didn't ever convince me that I needed to try to always be good. Let me show you what I mean.

If I say that the answer to "why be good?" is "so that I can return to my Heavenly Father," it's pretty easy to then start talking about repentance. We all know people who have messed up . . . they've gone to the parties and then some. But then they repent and things seem to be okay. Repentance is real, and it is absolutely there for us when we mess up. But if your "why," your reason for being good, is only so that you can return to your Father in Heaven, and you know about repentance, it's dangerously easy to justify messing up every now and then.

If I say that the answer to "why be good?" is "so that I can receive blessings," it's pretty easy to start thinking about rewards. But we all know people who do the right thing and DON'T get the immediate reward—or don't even seem to get the long-term reward. Some blessings are delayed. I have a friend who chose to STOP being good because she was tired of not seeing her "reward" for righteousness. And so if your "why" is only so that you can receive blessings, you end up constantly looking for proof that it pays to be good. And what happens when the "proof" you're looking for doesn't come soon enough?

That is why neither of those "why" answers is very foolproof, especially during your teenage years when there often aren't immediate consequences for your decisions.

I have to tell you that I know plenty of girls who messed up in high school, who seemed to have a lot of fun, and who later married in the temple. There was a time when that seemed so unfair. It's true that no one can really know the personal pain they might have gone through to get their lives back on track, but if we went just by appearances it would be easy to ask "why" over and over again based on how their lives turned out.

Eventually, my "why be good" answer—the answer I had to let sink deep into my heart in order to choose the right when it seemed to be more fun or easy to choose the wrong—was deeper. It had to be.

Answer these questions:

If you go to church, why do you?

If you pay your tithing, why do you?

If you honor your parents, why do you?

If you obey the Word of Wisdom, why do you?

If you stay away from pornography of any kind, why do you?

Now, think about something you participate in, like a sport or a talent or an extracurricular activity. It needs to be something that you spend time on, that you practice hard, that you give an effort to that has no assurance of a payoff. For example, you can work hard at a sport and still not win a championship. You can develop a talent and still not win a contest. You can spend time with an extracurricular activity at school and still not get a scholarship.

But you do it, right? You still work hard. You still spend time. You are still committed. WHY?

The answer is likely because you love it. There is something about just doing it that makes you feel good. You might love being a part of a team. You might love feeling like you are making a difference. You might love the recognition. But, when all is said and done, you do it because you love it, even if there is no guaranteed payoff.

John 14:15 (one of the easiest scriptures to memorize) says, "If ye love me, keep my commandments." And that, my friends, is my "why be good?" answer. It's the ONLY foolproof answer for me. Ultimately God wants us to obey him NOT out of duty or obligation, not out of fear, not because we hope to get some reward or blessing . . . but because we love Him.

It's as if He is saying:

"If ye love me, don't look at pornography."

"If ye love me, don't take a sip of that drink."

"If ye love me, walk out of the vulgar movie, even if you have to walk out alone."

"If ye love me, dress modestly."

IF YE LOVE ME.

When I am faced with a difficult choice (and those choices don't end after high school, by the way), the ONLY reason for me to choose the right over the wrong is BECAUSE I LOVE HIM. And that reason makes the other reasons (returning to live with Him and receiving His blessings) mean even more!

✳ little message ✳

Are there some things you should be doing that are hard for you to do? Are there things that you shouldn't be doing that are hard for you not to? Make a commitment list. Choose just two things that you will work on. Write them down in your journal or on a card that you keep in your scriptures. Use this language: "I will (or will not) _____ only because I love Him." And when you are faced with a difficult choice with that hard thing, think about or read your commitment sentence. It really works!

 **His Message to You**

BIG MESSAGE

It started out as just a chip in my windshield, a mark caused by the smallest of rocks. Did you know that if you catch a chip in time, the repair shop can put in a clear substance that seals the chip so it doesn't spread any farther? You really can't even see the chip after the repair.

But I had been so busy, and it seemed like such a little thing. I knew I could let it go for just a little while longer. Unfortunately, I waited too long.

What started out as a little chip spread almost overnight to become a three-foot-long crack across the middle of the window. I was so frustrated with myself! I was going to have to replace the entire windshield! If I had taken care of it when it was just a little chip, it would have cost me twenty dollars and maybe ten minutes.

Now, because it was such a big crack, it was going to cost more like two hundred dollars and a full hour.

Shortly after the chip turned into a crack, I was driving with some young women in my ward on an activity night. One of them noticed the crack (well, of course she did! It was THREE FEET LONG!!) and asked how it happened. But it wasn't me that answered her; it was the Spirit.

And here is what the Spirit taught me and the girls in my car that night:

We all sin. Some of these sins are "small" or "private" and can be taken care of between us and the Lord. Some of them are bigger and might involve another person. We might need to apologize or make amends to them (like when you hurt someone's feelings or "help" spread a rumor about another girl at school). And some sins are serious enough that we can't make things right without additional help. For times like that, the Lord has given us good bishops to talk to so they can help us make things right . . . repair the chip.

When you've done something serious enough to talk to the bishop about, you usually know it. Have you had the nagging feeling and the uneasiness that just won't leave? That feeling comes from the Spirit and helps you be unsettled enough that you'll take action. Be grateful for that feeling. Don't ignore it.

That nagging, unsettling feeling is like the little chip in the windshield. If you humbly go to your Father in Heaven in prayer and ask Him to help you have the courage to talk to your bishop, you can STOP further damage. You can "repair the chip." You can even repair it so it can't be seen!

But if you delay taking care of the sin, what was a little chip can become a much bigger crack (and, like with my windshield, it seems to happen overnight). Sure, the windshield can still be repaired (or replaced), but it will end up costing you more . . . more pain, more time, more unsettled moments without the peace of the Spirit.

Is there a "chip" in your life? It might have been caused by the smallest of rocks (or mistakes). Have you talked to Heavenly Father about it? If you are still feeling that nagging—if it still feels like the chip hasn't quite been repaired—talk to your bishop. Tell him your concerns. Let him help you fix that chip in your windshield before it becomes a much bigger crack.

I promise you won't even see that chip anymore . . . once it gets repaired.

✳ little message ✳

Part of the reason we pray every night is to check in with our Father in Heaven about our day and where we are with our lives. Ask Him to let you know if there is anything you need to take care of with Him or your bishop. Get anything cleared up that you might need to and give yourself the gift of peace.

His Message to You

section seven

JST U W8!

"Ye cannot behold with your natural eyes, for the present time, the design of your God concerning those things which shall come."

DOCTRINE AND COVENANTS 58:3

BIG MESSAGE

Some girls give me a hard time because when I speak I often say, "This is my favorite scripture," or, "I just have to share this favorite scripture," or, "I know I already told you my favorite scripture, but this one REALLY is."

And so, I won't say this is my FAVORITE, but it's definitely my favorite right now. The New Testament is full of real gems, and this is perhaps the gemmiest. (Yes, that is a word . . . at least it is now!)

"Him that is able to do EXCEEDING ABUNDANTLY above all that we ask or think, according to the power that worketh in us" (Ephesians 3:20; emphasis added).

WOW. Read that again.

I love that it's not talking about the Lord as "Him who is able to do just *a little bit* above all that we ask or think." It doesn't even say

"Him who is able to do *a lot* above." It says *exceeding abundantly* above. Do you know how much that is? That is more than a little . . . it's more than a lot . . . it's quite a lot more than a lot, in fact.

So, what does this mean for you?

Think of something that you really hope for . . . something you've asked for . . . something you really desire. And I'm not talking about that cute boy in math class talking to you (though that can certainly be something you really hope for)! I'm not talking about getting a car for your sixteenth birthday (though that might be something you've really asked for). I'm not even talking about getting a scholarship to the college of your choice (though certainly that is a worthy thing to desire).

I'm talking about *all* the things that are in your heart—all the things you've prayed for, asked for, thought of. Now imagine being granted that thing you've prayed for, asked for, thought of. NOW imagine getting EVEN MORE than that.

He can do that.

He WILL do that.

It might not be given to you quite how you asked for it, or quite how you thought of it, but I can promise you that what He has waiting for you is better than what you can imagine. Yes, even EXCEEDING ABUNDANTLY above.

Doesn't that make you smile?

Doesn't that get you excited?

He isn't just able to do a little of what you want or need. He isn't able to just do a lot of what you want or need. He is able to do "EXCEEDING ABUNDANTLY above all" that you think.

And then the next part is equally great: "according to the power that worketh in us." What power? HIS power. You are HIS daughter and, as such, you carry a part of His divinity within you. Whatever He is able to do for you, He is able to do because of your commitment and your works. He can magnify all of your efforts to help you be the girl and then the woman you want to become.

Exceeding abundantly above.

I LOVE the sound of that.

✻ little message ✻

Start your dream list of things you REALLY want in life. This shouldn't be a temporal list, but a list of things that really matter. Next to each dream, write a couple of commitments of what YOU will do to work towards that dream. Copy the scripture in Ephesians 3:20 and keep it with your list. Your dream list will likely change throughout your life as you start to see where Heavenly Father wants you and what He has prepared for you. But everything starts with a dream.

His Message to You

BIG MESSAGE

Think about the last time you went to any kind of celebration involving fireworks. Did the show start out with the biggest, coolest formation and explosion, and then the fireworks got smaller as the show continued? Of course not! Can you imagine the letdown? Instead, the fireworks show always starts with a few cool things here and there, but then the last few minutes you almost can't even breathe because it's so spectacular. The finale is supposed to be just that . . . a finale!

I love lying on the ground underneath a fireworks show. I love the beat of my heart that seems surprised at every "boom." I love to hear the "oohs" and the "ahhs" of the crowd (I'm usually the loudest "ooh-er" and "ahh-er" of them all). There's something so exciting about knowing it's going to build up to something really, really great. And the wait always seems to be worth it.

Another of my favorite scriptures is "Better is the end of a thing than the beginning thereof . . ." (Ecclesiastes 7:8). I'm a believer in that. I think that even if what you're experiencing right now is pretty great, what comes next will be even better. AND, happily, if what you're experiencing right now is sad or hard, what comes after it will be even better. That's true for this time that we live in too.

As amazing as some of the moments in our world's history have been—Adam and Eve starting their family, Noah and his family finding dry ground, Lehi and his family coming to America, the birth of Jesus Christ, Joseph Smith kneeling in a grove of trees—all of those moments have been building up to the ultimate moment: the Second Coming of the Lord Jesus Christ. Better IS the end of a thing.

This is such an important time to be alive. We have been told that these are the last days and that we have been chosen to help prepare the world for the amazing return of the Savior. Sister Elaine Dalton, Young Women general president, said, "Your coming to the earth now has been anticipated since the plan was accepted. Your position in time and place is no accident" (*Ensign,* May 2008, 116).

Think about a fireworks show and the anticipation of the finale. There have been great young women alive throughout all time. But THIS is it. This is the finale, the last few minutes, with nothing but spectacular moments one right after the other. Those moments are made up of YOU. Imagine the "oohs" and "ahhs" that might be coming from the heavens as they stand in wonder at all the incredible things you are helping to do.

This is such an exciting time to be alive.

This is it.

The finale.

Your "spectacular moment" is waiting for you.

✳ little message ✳

What would happen if you woke up every morning wondering what you were meant to do TODAY? What would happen if you approached each new day as one day closer to the coming of the Savior? In your morning prayers, ask Heavenly Father to help you see what He needs you to do that day. And then go about your day looking for things that were put in your path so that YOU could help create a spectacular moment.

His Message to You

section eight

:)

"If ye know these things, happy
are ye if ye do them."

JOHN 13:17

BIG MESSAGE

I had a lot of great teachers in Primary when I was growing up. I'm a believer that basically everything we need to know in life, we actually DO learn in Primary. "Say your prayers. Read your scriptures. Follow the prophet." Those answers are always the "right" answers to every question. Primary is pretty important!

But one teacher in particular, Sister Alfano, taught me a little bit more than just the "right" answer to every question. Somehow she convinced me that I was Heavenly Father's favorite. Really. I believed that He had favorites AND I believed that I was actually one of them. I totally remember thinking that if I was praying, Heavenly Father was listening only to me. If I was home from school sick, Heavenly Father was watching me at the house and not paying attention to any of the other kids. I didn't understand how

He could be present everywhere. In my little Primary mind, He could only really care for and watch over one, and for some reason I was the lucky kid. (Well, of course, because I was His favorite!)

As I got older and started having different experiences in life, I began to realize I couldn't possibly be His favorite. If I was, then "this" wouldn't have happened, or "that" WOULD have. And then I went on my mission and taught people the truth that they had a Father in Heaven who loved them. And I realized He had too many children to love and He simply couldn't have favorites. If He didn't have favorites at all, then that squashed the hope that I could possibly be one of them.

One day, while studying the scriptures, I opened the topical guide to "Favor, Favored" and I started to read some of the scriptures listed:

Samuel was in favor with the Lord (1 Samuel 2:26)

So shalt thou find favor in the sight of God (Proverbs 3:4)

Good man obtaineth favor of the Lord (Proverbs 12:2)

Mary: thou hast found favor with God (Luke 1:30)

Jesus increased in favor with God (Luke 2:52)

Could it be that Heavenly Father really does have children He favors? Not that He loves some children more than others . . . but

FAVORS some. And if He DOES have favorites, could I become one of them again?

Then I found this in the Book of Mormon: "He that is righteous is favored of God" (1 Nephi 17:35). I was a little discouraged because in my mind righteous = perfect. But, a few verses later, after Nephi was talking about how much the Lord blesses and loves the righteous, I read this: "He loveth those who will have him to be their God" (17:40). He favors the righteous. And the righteous are those who would have Him to be their God.

As I read that, I had two questions come into my mind.

Do I want my Father in Heaven to be my God?

Does He know it?

You choose Him to be your God when you choose to walk out of an inappropriate movie.

You choose Him to be your God when you choose to sit by someone unpopular at school.

You choose Him to be your God when you choose to say "I'm sorry" first.

You choose Him to be your God when you choose to buy a modest dress for the school dance.

The second sentence in the Young Women theme is a

declaration to the world that "we will stand as witnesses of God at all times, and in all things, and in all places." When you stand as His witness, you are choosing Him to be your God. He sees that. He knows that. He favors that.

So if someone ever asks you if God has favorites, you say "yes."

If they ask you who one of God's favorites is, you say "me."

(But make sure to wink when you say it so no one thinks you're obnoxious.)

Study it for yourself if you want to know if it's true. I want to believe Sister Alfano was right. I want to believe I AM Heavenly Father's favorite . . . well, one of them anyway.

✳ little message ✳

Look at the references under "Favor" in the Topical Guide. Commit some of your scripture study time to this topic. Make little notes with the scriptures you find and give them anonymously. Help others learn that they can be Heavenly Father's favorites too!

His Message to You

BIG MESSAGE

One of my favorite stories from Sister Elaine Dalton is her experience of running up "Heartbreak Hill" during the Boston Marathon. There's a reason it's called "Heartbreak Hill"—because it's the hardest part of the race. As she was running up the hill, she was feeling so alone. But right when she needed encouragement, there were people all along the way cheering her on. People she didn't even know (see *Ensign,* May 2008, 116–18).

When I heard her relating this experience, I started thinking of someone I did know—my friend Pam.

Sometimes in life we have hard moments. Maybe a time like that is a trial of our faith or a trial of our obedience. And when we are feeling alone, it just gets harder. But if you have someone cheering you on, or encouraging you, or helping you, it's so much easier.

I remember being at a friend's house with a bunch of girls from school. One of the girls started a movie, and I knew immediately that this wasn't a movie I should be watching. I sat there (my first mistake) and kind of buried my head in a pillow, feeling sick to my stomach but not knowing what to do.

I finally got up to use the rest room. Well, really, I got up so I could go find a place to say a prayer. I knelt right there at the toilet and told Heavenly Father about the situation. I told Him I knew I shouldn't be there but I didn't know what to do . . . these girls were my friends and I didn't want to be alone.

I got up and went back into the room (my second mistake). As soon as I sat down, my friend Pam turned to me and said, "Do you want to go play a game or something?" I have NEVER felt such relief. Together we got up and left the room. And in time, a few other girls came in and joined us.

I think about that experience a lot. I assumed I was all alone in my desire to not watch that movie. Little did I know that Pam didn't want to watch it either. But I needed her encouragement to do the right thing that night. It was like I felt alone on my own little

"Heartbreak Hill." And Pam was there to encourage me through HER courage to do the right thing.

When you were baptized, you made some important covenants with Heavenly Father. In addition to covenanting to be nice to others, you also made a covenant to support them—and not just when someone is feeling sad or needs comfort. You covenanted to "bear one another's burdens, that they may be light" (Mosiah 18:8). When you are in the moment of peer pressure, it feels heavy— really heavy. And when you're getting ready to submit to that peer pressure, the heaviness becomes darkness. I can't think of any better way to help bear someone's burden than to help them out of the heavy darkness.

That's what Pam (a girl very committed to her Baptist faith) and so many other amazing girls have done for me throughout my life. And I've made a promise to try to do that for them.

Being the first to walk out of a movie that's inappropriate isn't just the courageous thing to do, it's the KIND thing to do for the other friends who want to walk out too.

Telling a bunch of "mean girls" to stop talking badly about another girl at school isn't just the bold thing to do, it's the NICE thing to do for the other girls who want the talking to stop too.

Not letting a boy kiss you longer than is appropriate isn't just the brave thing to do, it's the SWEET thing to do for his sake and his connection with the Spirit. You're helping his burden be lighter. You're honoring your baptismal covenant by helping him honor his.

When I think about doing the right thing as being a way to show love to others, it totally changes my motivation. And that then influences my ability to do things that previously seemed hard to do.

I've been blessed with a lot of good friends. But no friend was ever more valuable to me than friends like Pam . . . girls who made my burden lighter by having the courage to "stand as a witness" and then invited me to stand with them. Want to experience some real happiness? Be the best kind of friend there is . . . be a Pam on Heartbreak Hill.

✳ little message ✳

Find a little heart-shaped charm you can wear on a bracelet or necklace when you're at school or out with friends. When faced with a temptation or peer-pressure situation, think of Heartbreak Hill.

Standing up with courage the first time is hard, but after you do it once, you'll find it easier the next time . . . and the next. Invite some of your other friends to join you, and none of you will feel alone.

His Message to You

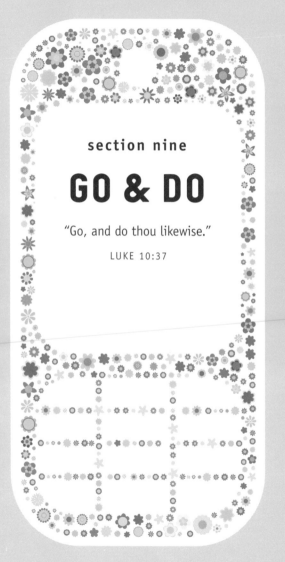

section nine

GO & DO

"Go, and do thou likewise."

LUKE 10:37

BIG MESSAGE

Have you ever wanted to be part of a revolution? I always thought it sounded so romantic. I liked to imagine participating in some grand revolution like in *Les Mis* where I boldly stood in front of the firing brigade waving the flag of my country. I could imagine maybe getting shot for my bravery but having some great writer turn my story into a stirring, award-winning musical. Was that too dramatic?

By definition, a revolution is "a radical and pervasive change in society and the social structure." And if any society or culture needed a radical change, it would be the one we're living in now.

In 2005, speaking to the young women of the Church, President Thomas S. Monson said: "You are an example of righteousness in a world which desperately needs your influence and your strength. . . . Today, permissiveness, immorality, pornography, and the power of peer pressure cause many to be tossed on a sea of sin and crushed on the jagged reefs of lost opportunities, forfeited blessings, and shattered dreams. . . . *Never underestimate the far-reaching influence of your testimony.* You can strengthen one another; you have the capacity to notice the unnoticed. When you have eyes to see, ears to hear, and hearts to feel, you can reach out and rescue others of your age" (*Ensign,* May 2005, 112–16; emphasis added).

I believe, if you're willing, you can be part of a grand revolution when the time comes. But guess what? I also believe the time is NOW!

I've spent time with so many young women these past few years. I have seen firsthand your goodness and your strength. You are part of the best generation that has ever lived. And you are needed. WOW, are you ever needed.

Once you know that you are a daughter of your Heavenly Father and that He loves you; once you know that you can talk to Him at any moment through prayer; once you know that He can talk to you through His holy scriptures; once you know the reason for choosing to follow His commandments; once you know He has

grand things waiting for you; and once you know that the only happiness you can ever truly find is by being the girl you were BORN
TO BE . . . there is still something left to do.

Your Father in Heaven needs strong girls to stand up and share
these truths with His other children. Are you ready?

There are so many ways you can share your testimony—your
light—and these truths with your friends and peers. You need to
prayerfully ask in what ways He needs YOU to join the revolution.

But here's one way to get you started:

Maybe God doesn't yet choose to text us directly, but maybe
He *would* choose to talk to some of His other children by texting
. . . through you. So, here's the challenge.

Save these text messages in your phone:

LYFSGUD

GOD LVS U!

24/7

U READ 2DAY?

B NYS 2 OTHRS

CTR

JST U W8!

:)   (I bet you already have this one in there!)

Choose one message each week to send out and invite your friends to forward. Start with the saved message on your phone (e-mail works too) and then add your own little inspirational thought. You might not know who will need it or even who will end up getting it, but share a message that you might hope to get yourself. You have more power to do good and help your friends BE good than most other influences. Just like President Monson said, "You can reach out and rescue others of your age."

It's time for a revolution of goodness.

Let's go . . . and do.

✳ little message ✳

I'd love to hear about what you do to share your testimony. If you choose to text or e-mail an inspirational message, I'd love to hear about it. (And if you come up with other inspirational text phrases, send them to me!) If you prayerfully discovered some other way, I'd love to hear about that too. Visit me at **GoAskLaurel.com** to share your experience and see what other girls just like you are doing. I can't promise any dramatic musicals will be written about our little revolution, but my heart tells me that what we experience together will be better than anything we could ever see on the stage.

His Message to You

About the Author

Laurel Christensen grew up in California, Kentucky, and Missouri. She holds a bachelor of science degree from Brigham Young University, which she received after serving in the Riverside California Mission. She has spent most of her career at Deseret Book Company, where she worked for several years as the director of entertainment, producing shows like *The Forgotten Carols* and launching and managing Jericho Road, among other artists. She is currently the general manager for the Time Out for Women division and spends many weekends on the road producing Time Out events. Laurel recently completed a master's program in communications management and hopes to take the LSAT soon, just to say she did it. She loves working with teenage girls and especially likes making sure they are well educated about the world of Jane Austen. She has released two talk CDs: *God Knows You're Amazing* and *Who's That Girl?*

✳ Have a question? ✳

Visit **GoAskLaurel.com**

"I might not know the answers, but I know where to look . . ."